ACKNOWLEDGEMENTS

A number of these poems have appeared in the following publications:

DANDELION	PAPERBAG POEMS
FREELANCE	PORTICO
GRAIN	QUARRY
MALAHAT REVIEW	VORTEX
NEWEST REVIEW	WAVES
ORIGINS	

Some of the poems have been broadcast on Alberta Anthology, CBC Anthology, and Access Radio CKUA.

The publisher gratefully acknowledges the assistance of The Canada Council and The Saskatchewan Arts Board in the publication of this book.

The Life of Ryley

Monty Reid

THE LIFE OF RYLEY © copyright 1981 by Monty Reid

ISBN 0-920066-39-9 (paper)
ISBN 0-920066-40-2 (cloth)

Book design by Neil Wagner

Published Fall 1981 by

Thistledown Press
668 East Place
Saskatoon, Sask.
S7J 2Z5

Canadian Cataloguing in Publication Data
    Reid, Monty, 1952 -
        The Life of Ryley

        Poems.
        ISBN 0-920066-40-2 (bound).
        ISBN 0-920066-39-9 (pbk.)

        I. Title.
        PS8585.E43L5   C811'.54   C81-091135-3
        PR9199.3.R43L5

for Pat

TABLE OF CONTENTS

The Road Back and Forth to Ryley

The mist splits open for light the way the heart
is parted for clarity. On the fields
at the edge of town white-tail browse
dark air damp on their pelage. Morning
edges down the road behind us and we've
forgotten the camera, as we always do when
deer are there, but always have it when dead skunks
and porcupines lie on the shoulders, entrails
plucked by magpies, ravens, unphotogenic crows.
Or we're late for work and can't stop.
The deer lift their heads but don't run
and the ground goes fluent with dawn.

Or the dark in mid-winter.
Through the moraine at Cooking Lake
where glaciers off the mountains and the shield
met and ground slowly into one another.
Now the snow through aspens that cover
the hummocks of till. Cones of light.
Drifts climb from the ditches, sprawl
unself-consciously over the road and we follow
the snowplow at thirty mph not
seeing anything except the blue light
diffract in white.

The girls they have for flagmen wave you down.
Euclids belly along the roadbed, the dirt
all ruts or hung in the air like an allergy
and it's summer, the girls in hardhats and
haltertops, shoulders flushed with
sun. All you can see is dust. Or farther
past the construction, where heat wraps the highway
in cellophane, the way things are packaged
so you don't see what you've got til you've paid
for it. But I could drive this road
blindfolded.

The city hoists itself into light
block by block on threads of smoke
and the traffic thickens, bumper to bumper
all the way in from Sherwood Park and when one stops
everybody does. If you were with me
you'd be nervous, stiffening every time
someone merged ahead of us, your foot
pumps an imaginary brake.
                              At night, from Ryley
the city's glare floats on the horizon like the nest
of a waterbird. In the morning, driving,
it disappears.

Commuters

Heat opens eyes
on the windshield.

Your breath hits it
fogs and
disappears.

The cold comes up
to the glass to
look in.

Last night at the upstairs
window you melted a hole
in the frost with your fingertips.
They came away white
as headlights.

Now
we wait for the van
to warm up
you shiver
in the appearing air.

On the street
cars approach
and vanish

and in this magic
the eyes open wide with
amazement.

Blackout

All the motors quit: furnace,
deepfreeze, fridge, tv dead
in the middle of Battlestar Galactica.
In the sudden quiet of the house
they run into each other, grope
for flashlight, matches, candles.
Then they surround the light
like planets.

The kids crowd the candle with dreams
of space. They watch lights
in the windows of other houses,
feeble as stars, talk about ships
going into freefall, hyperspace
but won't move. When the candle
burns down he goes to find another
stumbling through the dark. A voice
behind a hand. When he comes
downstairs he steps on something
and it breaks; in the kitchen
the kids groan.

And a minute later the lights go on
the kids want to phone to see
if the power was off at their friend's
place too. He blows the candle out.
No one mentions the Star Trek model
shattered at the foot of the stairs.

Meeting Hutterites

I

Rumor has it
they're inbred
they bring in
males to lock
in the colony
shed overnight
with all the
cross-eyed girls.

New blood.

And now
at the door
a girl in
a black skirt

jars of honey
in a tray.

II

I remember how
my uncle axed the heads
off chickens
the spouting neck
beating
into shed walls.

I was always afraid
of the bird flying
into me.

And now they come
to the door
with their sack
of headless frozen birds.

The wind lifts
their scarves like
wings.

III

An accident we saw once:

    a two-ton
upside down in the ditch
with bags of fertilizer broken
and spread on the road like dead birds.

We could smell gas leaking as we pried
at the doors with a crowbar.
                        Inside, they
were pounding their hands against the metal.

When we got them out there was blood
on their black pants.
                  It was cold.
They were shaking and went back to scrape
the sacks off the road with borrowed shovels.

IV

Black

they stand
in the snow
like print
on a page.

Is that why I think of death?

Once when the school
toured the colony
the Hutterite kids
followed us around

singing.

Shuffleboard
(for Danny Desorlais)

Standing at the end of a table
that stretches away under the lights
like a city street, the flawless
rocks in his hand, the almost
irresistible urge to throw them
to try their weight against drywall,
plywood, glass.

But he keeps them on the board
banking them impeccably around guards
the rocks spinning silently on the sand
hanging like acrobats over the edge
for more points.

Easy money he says.
Easy money he shouts later
when he's drunk and the shots
are accurate out of confidence
and habit, the numbers punched out
into the lit squares above the board.
Play you for a buck he says.
Easiest money I'll ever make.

And the red rocks
follow the green rocks in
playing takeout now because
he's lost his draw weight
fumbling with the buttons
as though the body of light
embarrassed him but he
wins, everyone else
as drunk as he is.

He walks home
with the bills crumpled in his shirt pocket
weaving back and forth on the sidewalk
past the streetlights and the lights
left on in the locked-up stores
and when he falls down on his bed the room
spins until he falls off the edge
into the sand of dreams.

Look at You

You're so drunk
one says
you have to close

one eye
just to see
straight

and

yeah but it
don't do no
good

when you close
one eye
you just see

twice as much
with the other.

Two drunks
in the Ryley bar

and I have heard
of Milton blind

and Creeley
sitting
at a typewriter

with only
one eye.

Test Drive

(for Jack and Leona)

It's spring, the roads
full of frost heaves and pot-holes
but you don't feel them. The shocks
compress. In the backseat
the salesman holds on to the armrest
and winces. There's a lot
of protection there in case you have
an accident he says; the clouds
reflect in the long hood. It feels
like you're riding on air. Through
the sunroof we watch the high flights
of Canada geese drift through their
flyways. We explore the electric
windows and remote-control mirrors
and barely notice the image: ducks
that nest at the roadside launched
into the air. A stupid panic
when we drive so noiselessly
by.

The Last Daughter Leaves Home

Drawn
as a wishbone
is drawn

to those
known or
secret wishes

this family
is spread.

Susan
in a chicken joint
these faces
greased by tears

in a spattered
kitchen and
for minimum
wage

her
hands pluck
that slim bone
from my chest.

Complaint of the Road-Repair Man

I get tired scratching your back.
Put me on the shovel all day,
but put me here beside you,
my nails on the scars and the vertebrae,
on the ribs that come up
sturdy as overpasses from your heart,
and my arm hurts. Yesterday it rained
and we stayed in the shop. My feet
soak up cold from the concrete floor,
come home aching.
We bolted the scarifier on the grader,
teeth that tear the highway up,
and tomorrow if it's nice
we're going to rip the surface
off that road.

Her Story

I was born in a hospital in a small town
    beside a large shallow lake. My mother
said while she lay there, between the spasms of
    pain, she could hear the hard
flights of mallard and pintail, avocets, bittern
    heron, the ragged v's of Canada geese
come flailing in to the mudflats and reed beds
    around the lake. When I cried they may have
heard me there, the birds gathering on the shore
    before migration.

Once I had appendicitis and there were no birds
    but once, when I was getting my tonsils
out, I lay propped up on the pillows and watched
    the gulls, herring and ring-billed and California
even a glaucous, strut around the incinerator
    pecking at scraps of garbage
generals plotting a coup.

Later, my eldest son being born
    prematurely into the world and the birds
were there then. In fact, we had been out hunting
    and it may have been the squatting in the cold
blind while the mist came off the lake like a wool
    sweater, the steel of the shotgun ice
against my cheek, that brought the birth
    on early. Or it may have been the excitement, the gun
bruising my shoulder, the weight of ducks
    we carried back to the truck, or it may simply
have been the smallness of my body and its inability
    to carry full term. But he was early.
We weren't sure he would live. And the birds
    were there then too. I dreamt them tumbling
shot out of the sky above the hospital.

I live now near the lake I was born beside.
    The kids aren't that interested in birds.
I watch the herons and cranes and storks
    flap over and my husband yells at the gulls
that shit on the fence he's just painted.
    I sometimes think the birds are crazy
to keep coming back to this lake
    tho I love watching them
and I also know
    they can't help it.

Pit Run

"All it is
is an old slough, that stretch from the hospital
east. I went over that fucking road twice a day
every day last week and it didn't do a damn bit a good.
What we gotta do is rip it right outa there and put a couple
loads a pit run in there. You just doze them big rocks,"

he circles his hands above his head.

"A couple a times and the cocksuckers sink right down.
You can see em going.
You know them pilings for that hospital or lodge or
whatever the hell it is they're building there, they were
sposed to be 12 feet deep well they hadda go 21 before
they hit anything solid. It's that fucking soft."

It's raining again. We nod our heads over coffee.
When we came in for work this morning there was a new
crack in the shop floor, cement settling. And Steve
left the window open in the crewcab and it's soaked.
The gradermen from Viking are here to pick up parts.

"All you guys do is bitch,"
                    Merv says.
"If you worked half as much as you talked
those roads'd be in great shape."
                    We laugh
and wreck the stirsticks with our fingernails.

At night I hear the trucks pass on the highway.
I know they're full of stones and clay. They look
for a soft spot in the middle of a country road
to dump it in. They fade, the night
blades them under. I dream like a mechanic
in a shop full of cold feet and power tools
and big country radio. And in the morning,
wake to rain.

Skidooers

The big jack stretches and unstretches
towards the fence, the movement of a heart
contract, expand, floating across
the snow.

Six of us: two Kawasakis, two Yammies,
one John Deere, one old SkiRoule with
high loops welded onto the front of the skis
so he can go over wire.

The jack breaks for the scrub
angling off for the fenceline and we
swing in behind him, thighs sore against
the machine's push, trying to intersect
the jack's line to the fence.

But he can run.
We pull up beside, the black eyes not moving
the legs bunching, thrusting, but he's too
close to the fence and we can't cut him off.

So we pull up, except for Stan
on one of the big Yamahas, riding in close
to the rabbit and trying to stare him down
and hit the fence at it must have been
close to fifty.

One strand slicing through the fibreglas
cowling and then snapping, the other rides
up over the windscreen, catching Stan across the armpits
one barb hooked into the nylon suit
standing up because the sudden stopping was lifting
him up and forwards and the wire takes him
across the chest, whipping him off the machine
backwards into the snow.

And the jack running and the machine running
the throttle jammed open
and Stan lying in the snow
a spot of blood under his nose.

Groceries

The packages slide
past: cellophane and tin,
and the teller pokes the register
the way she'd poke a fat
man in the ribs. You're
missing one; she totals
up our bones.

I remember peaches.
I took one off the store
display and ate it as we
filled our cart.
The store detectives caught
us at the checkout.
They never said much
but I could taste that peach
for days.

Spring Ease

In March the waxwings picked the shrivelled berries
off the ash tree. The cat twitched at the window
and the grey clouds edged under the horizon.
Slow month. Now the birds turn on the wind
that whips the clouds from the sky, the cat
scratches at the door. The girl, whose eyes
also are grey, who says the kitchen's hot,
lets the cat out as she herself leaves for a walk
among the hills, hunting for crocus. April.
May. The boys work overtime. She sits on the hill's
south face, a flower in her hand.
Now there is only desire, warm
ground. Her eyes follow the cloud over
the hills. Sun and wind flush her face
as love would. In the kitchen she sets the plates
on the tablecloth covered with flowers.
The men come in from the field
and don't notice.

The Shorebirds

Snowy owls still sit on the ice in the middle
of the lake, quiet as the arctic all afternoon
and in the evening hunt along the shore.
A muskrat pushes angles through the ring
of open water and among the cattails
dried out by winter a blackbird caws.
And I would have thought it too early
for geese but they spill out of their corners
in the sky and slap into the water. When
I come back the next day the owls are gone.

It starts that way: with disappearance.
The wrist of ice melts from the ring of
black water; bracelet swallows bone.
We stand on the soggy hummocks with cameras
and binoculars around our necks, watch
flights land on the flooded meadows,
the cold lake. These migrants
full of distance: snipe, plover,
whimbrel. They fill this empty
season with their noise.

Sometimes I think they don't trust the water,
these birds that live on the lake-edge.
Why else the long legs, the herons
four feet above the surface, drawn up
to protect a dignity that survives even
the frogs they pluck from grass blades.
Or the godwits on one leg like kids
with bootfulls. We watch from a blind
stitched together from reeds and bulrush
and mare's tail, tell ourselves the birds
don't see us, don't mind us here.

Needle beaks. The avocets pluck
midges off the mudflats. Parliaments
of knots and sandpipers legislate along
the margins of the lake. They vote
bugs into their mouths. Egrets from California.
Sometimes you see a banded leg, the capture
carried there like jewellery. We write
on them and try to set them free
and fail. Out of season, we watch
an owl, gone brown in the chest
drift soundlessly north.

For Barry and Noreen: who lost a finger

He counts the years off on his hand.
Living together for two, married
for two, a handful of fights, jobs,
screwing around, reconciliations.
And for this last year, when her father
died and left her the farm and they had to
drive out from the city to work it
there is no finger. For a while
they didn't know which way to turn.

The power-take-off took the thumb
counterclockwise, against the joint,
the mitt in the spinning steel
skin unwound in a spiral
halfway to the elbow and then
he was tossed out of it
before he had time to yell.

And when he lay in the hospital
with the thinned blood being pushed
through the sewn-on finger she told us
how she felt responsible, how he
wanted her to sell the farm.
She keeps her hands folded
in her lap, not moving.

And every night, on the hospital bed,
where he is propped at one end and
she sits cross-legged at the other,
their hands meet across the sheets,
his wrapped in gauze and plaster,
the thumb sticking through a hole
black and uncertain as cattails
sticking through the ice that heals
the sloughs every fall, hers pale,
manicured, her fingers touch
the thumb. Where it feels to him
that his hand is frozen and he can't
really be sure she touches him
it feels to her like bare skin
stuck to steel.

Cousins

I don't remember the names
of all the parts I handed up
to Brian as he lay half in the dusty hole.
Twelve years old and only wanting to be sure
that I was helping as he pulled
the beater bars from the clogged belly
of the old pulltype. They rotated backwards,
barley caught between them and the combine
had to stop every hundred yards just
to let them clear. Now we have it
in the yard: apart.
He had a plastic mask
over his face because he was allergic
to barley dust and I remember coughing too
and getting a rash on my elbows and neck.

Years later, and I still don't know
the names of things. We sit around
the suppertable and recall the few times
I helped on the farm, how I'd sulk
or try to sic the dog on the chickens
when they told me just to keep out of the way.
We examine the various partings
how I've worked in the city
for three or four years now and
Brian, like he does every time I see him,
has to ask, what was it
you said you did?

Necklace

When the dogs came home
they weren't interested in supper.
We could see them from the kitchen window
lying by the barn.

When we went to check the cattle
we found one dead, stiff
legs in the sky, a red hole
where the dogs had eaten
the udder away.

When we crept up to the house
with whatever had killed the cow
already tearing at their stomachs
we could see how far in
they'd stuck their heads

around their necks
a noose of blood.

Rock Tumbler

In the porch
small barrels turn
over and over
with pebbles in them.
The grit
wears the stone
down. Moon rocks
from India, agates,
they revolve
and fall, revolve
and fall, and
the edges disintegrate.
The kids have already
lost the cheap settings
the stones were to be
glued to: tie-clips,
rings. The instructions
said tumbling was just
like stream action
only speeded up.
The barrels turn all
night and I can hear
a river scraping
through the house.
A woman
fishes in the water
for a stone.

Fire Practice

Some fires you can't put out with water.
That's what they tell us, the volunteers,
when we come down to the station
for the first practice. Stiff rubber
coats hang on the far wall. Motionless
as guards, they wait for us to fit them.

We take the truck out
to the last hydrant at the edge of town
practice how to start the pump
how to fit the masks tight, how to
brace the nozzle against your chest
when the water pressure stiffens in
the hose and pulls you backwards.
It knocks Johnny over, he drops the hose
and we all get wet. All the time
we imagine fire.

At the end, we unreel
the hose, lifting it to run the water out.
Our coats are mud and ice. We laugh
because we got more water on ourselves
than anywhere else. As I wait
at the truck I see the luminous squares
taped on the backs of the slickers float
and glow in the darkness as volunteers
go back to check the hydrant one last time.
Above us the sky flares with aurora and
back at the station they tell us, some
fires, all you can do is contain them.
And hope you're insured.

Boat People

The dipper tilts in the north and spills
stars. Smoke from the stubble collects
in the ditches like water.
                        Today when we
drove Ahn Nhoc and his kids out from
the city they got scared: all of a sudden
pale hills, bare as the Plain of Jars.
They did not believe we lived here
or that the bush had anything in it
except a camp like the one they came from.
Only the traffic reassured them.
                        We left them
in half a duplex the church had ready for them
talking Cantonese to the lady from
the restaurant.
                        Now, going home,
the poplars in the ditch tilt through
smoke like spars of sinking junks.

And the stubble flares
like a ship
burning.

Washing Berries

"I don't feel like washing the berries
tonight."
          You scour the stains off your hands.
The water discolors and is gone. The kitchen
sink is full of saskatoons.
                    We could
spot the bushes from the road, top
heavy with berries. You wade through
the mud and weed in the ditch with
an old ice cream pail hooked to your belt.
You stamp down the thistles and try
to avoid the roses; somehow they
always touch you.
                    We pull the branches
down and dusty berries erupt into our hands.
I know my mouth is stained; yours is.

So what does one say if the berries don't get
washed tonight. The berries will keep. It
demands nothing. You hold the room
around you, as the flesh of berries fills
their skin. My hands are pale
where I scrubbed the purple off them.
They float like the weightless tufts
that carry seed from trees. The air
takes them, turning and turning
back to color.

The Return of Lassie

Remember when we use to live
in the city and saw nearly all
the movies that came to town?
And now we haven't seen one
since we took the kids to Viking
on their birthday for that stupid
show about a dog jumping
through a window filled with fire.
We used to read reviews; now
we never do. On the way home
a big german shepherd ran
out of a driveway at the car
and we slowed down and tried
to hit the bitch.

Walking to Dance

All winter we take social dance
fox-trot, rhumba, waltz, steps
in front of mirrors
practising alone to move together.

It snowed last night and today
it drops to -30. The van
won't start. So call Susan
say we'll walk to dance
and should leave early.

It is the only way of getting
there, single-file through
the drifts, through the shadows
of the spruce gone
white as crinolines.

They revolve and revolve
around us, their dance
without reflection
in the snow.

The Disposal of Hazardous Wastes

The cultivator unfolds the earth: old
letters. We read them again and again.
The shovels turn the worms up and they lie
like veins on the surface, stunned by light.
Dirt runs through them like blood.
When they move the birds get them,
pluck them in their beaks like string.

Here in the yard a nest of mouths
they stitch together. They stand
on the lip of twigs and dangle the worms.
Drop them, preen, and are gone.
They feed all day. The next they
follow the sprayer across the second
quarter, its booms spread out
for balance: tightrope
of earth.

The air takes the spray apart
and even though there is no wind
we can smell it. It hangs
in the yard like the must
of old papers bound with twine
and stacked in the basement.
What is it we write
to ourselves?

The day after, we found the gawky
bodies on the lawn. Plucked out,
veins blue with pesticide, transparent
skin. We picked them up and
threw them in the ditch. A cat
will probably find them. And as we
walked from the house to wherever
we could hear the birds, their songs
tumble over and over
out of the air.

Tractor Hour

Pat found the station the last time she
came out here. Driving home alone after dropping
the kids off, suitcases and a bagful of patching,
she said she wasn't used to the quiet. Around her
in the fields she could see the big four-wheel
drives unreel the earth behind them. Deep tillage.
They drag the heart up to the surface.
Behind her the highway stretched out like summerfallow.

And on the radio, turning the needle
back and forth past the local country
station and talkshows, the bible hour, past
the voices that fade in and out, overlapping.
What goes on in the air is so erratic.
She found the Tractor Hour, the dj taking
calls and dedicating songs to the guys out
in the cabs, talking fertilizer, wheat board,
machinery. The calls came in: "I'd like to
dedicate something by Waylon Jennings to my dad
who's out doing summerfallow on Hetland's old
quarter," or "Could you play Don't It Make my Brown
Eyes Blue for Don who's driving the Co-op bulk
truck today?" And every now and then, Pat could see
someone high in a cab with a set of headphones on.

She held the needle on that station until she
couldn't hear it any more. It went the way jeans
go, something showing through that looks like skin
and bone. Sometimes they're not worth fixing.
But a month later when we went to pick the kids
up, they were waiting for us, excited because Tom
let them drive his tractor and it even had a radio
and Grandma got the radio to play a song for them.
And David ripped his pants climbing into a steel
bin and Grandma had to sew them.

Driving home the next day
we listened to the Tractor Hour again
the car full of the usual human noise,
the radio's needle patching the sound
over us so that all we can do is look
at each other and hum the music
that's there.

The Old Ladies Take A Charter

Pills, bibles, hot water bottles;
they gather their wits about them.
All summer they consider excuses
but the cheap fares convert them.
Except Ida, who says she just can't
afford it, even with two pensions.
So she gets her house ready for winter
while the rest meet with the minister
and change their money. Pamphlets
and sandwiches. He remembers
the excuses they waved at him like
hymnals and prayerbooks and then
set them on the pew.

Now that's over.
The airplane waits like a house
of worship. They show their boarding
passes and the guard frisks them
and the earth falls away like a heresy.
Every week they sat through church
without transport; now this.
They tremble in the temple of their own
motion and gather their unimportance
to them like parachutes. They get
airsick. The attendant takes the bags
away.

Finally. Tel Aviv. The Holy Land.
They find ancient streets and kiss
them. Notes drummed on tambours.
Donkey tours. They lie under an umbrella
on the beach. Sun and basil.
Ida gets the postcards that say
wish you were here; the bales
are piled around her house like sand.

The Ladies Take a Walk in August

They patrol the alleys all summer.
Now there is a chill; they wrap
themselves in sweaters.

They pinch each other, nod, point
at the garden where the flowers
hold the coolness. A hummingbird

hangs from a hollyhock, its beak
stitches sweetness to it.
At the corner, kids with new

licences squawk their tires.
You could get dizzy trying to
follow the hummingbird. They watch

and shuffle up the alley, back
to the frugal kitchens, the houses
full of photographs and dream.

In the evening they patch their
sweaters. The light deflects off glass
and gloss paper;

an iridescence of wings.

The Ladies Gossip

Edna tells Molly and Molly tells
Chrissie and Chrissie tells Ida and Nora
gets it from her. So Nora
tells Susan and Susan tells Rita
and Donna, Janice, and Deb.
Meanwhile Molly phoned Josephine
who passed it on to Flo and Muriel
who told Louise and Val and Shirley.
Shirley told the girls at the office
and Louise told Wendy. Wendy told
Margaret who told Joyce who
told Leona. Gail rubbered in
when Leona called Alice and she
told Carol. Carol told Mildred
and Mildred even told her mother.
Her mother told Irene and Myrtle
when she had them in for coffee.
Alice told Mona. Myrtle told
Janice but Janice heard it a long
time ago. Irene told Ethel who
told Sylvia who told Diane who told
Donna, a different Donna.

48

Donna told Yvonne who told
her younger sister. Ethel
told Rita again but Rita
said she heard it different. Mona
finally decided to tell someone
and Audrey was so shocked she told
Dorothy who told Violet and Anne.
Anne told Betty and Daphne. It
got the whole town talking.
Betty told Agnes and Agnes told Wilma.
Somehow Miriam heard it. Ruth
found out from Cathy and told
Kay who told Bonnie. What
a bunch of gossips said Bonnie.
She told June. June told Darlene
who told Gloria. Gloria told Gwen
and Gwen told Jean and Jean went
and told Barb and Barb told Edna
and Edna said no you've got
the whole thing wrong. So Barb
went back and told Jean
who told Gwen who told Gloria
and someone told Pat
and even I heard it
and now since it's nice
to know how things get started
around here
I'm telling you.

The Crotchety Old Ladies Play Scrabble

They drink tea and eat
thin wafers and their dresses
are discreetly long. They draw
letters, arrange them into words
tag one word to another. The game
fits them like an old nightie.
Compulsion. I get such lousy
letters Ida says and every word
I make is just the one you need.
Her patience frays. Molly
is the other one. She's played
for years and has a long string
of victories but long strings end.
Says Ida. A dictionary by her hand.
She makes up her own rules.
Double letter, triple word, they
kill the afternoon with names.
There is no end to remembering.
If I could only get my letters out
they say. The tea goes bitter
at the end.

Loose Tooth

Corey wouldn't let us touch
his first loose tooth
for over two months,
not trusting our hands
for small enough motions.

He wiggled it with his tongue
and fingers, til it hung
by a thread, but couldn't
bring himself to pull
it out.

And then one day in the city
he swallowed it, with
a mouthful
of Big Mac.

Dishpan Hands

I touch you and you're
about as warm as dishwater.
Tonight I washed them for you
my hands in the water with
the peels and grease and
porridge that still
clogged the drain. Of course
I expected something for it.

And now in the moonlight
that spills like rinse water
from the tap in the sky
our bodies glisten like
wet plates standing in the rack.
At least mine does. Yours
lies unscraped and filmed
with soap. You can't hear me
through the water. And when
my chapped hands reach for you
all they touch is cutlery.

Taxing the Churches

We were in Lacombe staying with friends at Canadian Union College
an institution run by seventh-day adventists, when we first heard
about the jonestown massacre and we never brought the subject
up but understandably we got talking about suicide and cults and
Darlene said she'd heard a psychologist on the radio explaining
the popularity of these groups and the psychologist kept
comparing them to adventists.

But we're not that bad Darlene says. I mean sure, we've got Ellen G.
White and she used to go into fits and hold heavy bibles over her
head for hours and wrote all those predictions — which are coming
true even today — but she never killed anyone although she bores
me very close to death. I mean, jeez, the stars did fall in 1844 and
the moon turned to blood and all that and you can understand the
effect that would have on people. I wouldn't squirt cyanide into my
baby's mouth though.

But I remember the time I went to Walla Walla, another adventist
institution and in the philosophy of education class we were
talking about Harvey Cox and situation ethics and the question
arose:
what choice would you make if it came down to either breaking a
commandment or killing your children and almost the whole class
said they'd kill their kids.

After dinner, and Darlene is a good cook, not a vegetarian because she thinks all the adventist vegetarian food companies are ripping her off and that maybe there's a little collusion between the ministers and the nutritionists and she doesn't like the taste anyway, we sit around and wait for sunset while Byron tells me how he paid tithe out of his last paycheck 10% before deductions and how they keep building new general conference buildings and more elaborate churches and staffing them with ministers, youth leaders, organists, choirs, janitors, sunshine bands, pathfinders, you name it. And all the guys who can't make it as doctors or dentists or optometrists here always go to be missionaries in the far-off lands, as they say in sabbath school, and they live on Byron's money there too.

I remember looking for books on Marx in the library at CUC but there weren't any except one explaining in a chapter how Marx was wrong. There were more than three hundred works by or about Ellen G. White and how she's still right even today, although she did recommend that no one ride bicycles. But you can't take her out of context said Willis Clark who taught bible class, the same man who told us in grade 10 that the catholics already had the mark of the beast on their foreheads — 666 on one of the pope's various caps — and that these same catholics were building a hospital in Saskatoon and in the hospital were a lot of underground chambers they would use for the incarceration and torture of adventists when the time of persecution came.

So we go up to the alumni banquet where I meet so many old friends
who are gaining weight and financial respectability and are con-
ducting bible study groups wherever the lord calls them and are
having babies and there is no way I can deny that these are my
friends. And at the banquet they disclose further plans for the
expansion of the school and we all clap but there is some bad news
in that the universities amendment act hadn't been passed in the
legislature because some of the people associated with the worldly
universities were worried the new act might cheapen degrees a
little but I have every assurance says the speaker, that this is just
a formality, the minister in charge told me this himself,   we will
become a degree-granting institution within a year.

After supper we shake hands and sit around the lounge and just relax.

Somewhere in Guyana Jimmy Jones lies on the rostrum of his temple
bloated with the hot jungle air
and with salvation.

The Alumni Game at Lacombe Arena

Kindopp can't buy a goal.
Breaking in alone and fanning
or ringing a shot off the goalpost
from twenty feet. He chases his
own rebound into the corner
passes it behind the net
and when the puck comes back to him
someone lifts his stick.
When the defenceman walks in and scores
they don't even give Kindopp an assist.

After the game he pulls his skates off
drags the sweater over his head.
I'm getting too old for this game he says
if I had a dime for every chance I had . . . .
He strips and showers and flicks
the wet towel at his right winger.
It's not til he's half-dressed
and reaching for his comb
that he makes the discovery,
along with the rest of the team,
that someone left the dressingroom open
and his wallet's gone
and that he's not really worried
about the money
but he'd like the i.d. back.

Crawlspace

Why they built this house
with no basement is beyond me.
Just this space between the planks
of the floor and the ground, damp.
I go down on my belly to check
the pipes, the wiring and two
feet above me the kids run.
They take it for granted
there's nothing under them.
The way leaves fall. Except
in January when winter sits here
like an animal and the pipes freeze
and frost blooms on the foundation.
Then when they run they run
softly. But now the spiders
are the only things scared,
legging it out of crevices.
And I'm lying here with the troublelight
looking at the pipes, listening
to the lives passing overhead
and under me, where I wish
I had a basement, comes the rustling
breath of an animal that lives
in the ground and every time we move,
moves.

Pouring Cement at Helen's

Rye and water, half and half
or rye straight. Helen makes the drinks
and sets them on the table.
Today we poured cement around her house,
sidewalk and patio, and tomorrow
if it's cool we'll take the forms off.
For now though we're finished.
Floated, trowelled, the edging done,
a pattern put on the surface with a broom
so no one slips on it. We sit
around the table as Helen
and her daughters do the dishes,
scraping scraps into the garbage.
We slouch in our seats, or tilt
the chairs back, precarious as wheelbarrows.

And later Helen compares this house
to others she's lived in. No heat,
no water, no sidewalks. How the kids
all slept in one room, the parents
in another and the rest was kitchen.
How one night in February she got up
and had to go to the bathroom which was,
on that farm, about ten miles away, it
seemed like, and because nobody would get up
and go with her she thought she'd go
instead in the slop-pail under the sink.

The floor was freezing and she didn't
wear shoes because she didn't want anyone
to hear her. She got the half-full five
gallon pail out and instead of just sitting
on it she tried to hold it tilted under her
so she could pee against the side
and not make noise. It slipped.
She fell into the slop running on the floor,
the peels, the grease, the dirty water
dripping through the trapdoor
into the cellar and already freezing.
She had to wash her ass in the dishpan
and it took her most of the night
to scrape the mess off the floor.
But no one woke up.

We are thrown back in our chairs
roaring and Gary overbalances and slams
against the wall and after that
we all sit, in this house full of warmth
and light and modern comfort,
with four legs firmly on the ground.

Doing the Wiring

Loomex wove through the house.
He was tightening connectors in a junction box
when she leaned through the hole
he'd pulled the door from
saying "ready for lunch?"
He stepped onto the porch, into sun
coffee, sandwiches. But toggles
breakers, ground, he maps
the new circuit in his head.

She left, after gathering the thermos,
cellophane, the cookies he didn't want
and he went back to remodelling,
angry with himself for not talking to her.
Old spark, the limbs flexed
against him once on a visit two years
ago and his wife had told him,
"I think she has a crush on you."
They laughed: distance
is the best insulator.
Now she moves her body, touched
into amber by the sun, through
the altering space around him
while his wife is with friends
down the street.

No electrician, it took
all afternoon to hide the power
in the walls, to hook switches
to the wire-ends, burying the lines
of cause and effect in the studs
across the ceiling. In the evening
she is there again and he shows
off, flicking switches, preening
in the light tossed across filaments
room by room the house lit up.
She touches him on the arm
and in the light that makes the room look
so small they twist together like copper.
As copper is twisted together so the current
flows through and forgets it. The house
glows with light and unremembering.

For Nikayla

i

The bed pulses like a heart
valves pump a reminder
through the water she lies on
through the forgetful body:
                                    breathe

tubes, wires, electrodes,
needles, the irregular luxury
of a waterbed
                    among the metals
one livid spot.

The next baby pees all over the incubator
and the nurse moves by, dry,
nonchalant as gauze, steel, plexiglass, all
that apparatus of memory.

Alone in another room
Janice pumps milk into the bottles
she will bring to the hospital
imagining the small pull
of a mouth.

And here, Nikayla with a prong
in her nose for air
for the milk, a clear
tube to the belly.

Neo-natal intensive care
we stand in the hall
watch from behind reinforced glass
the simple poverty
of our breath.

ii

Convulsed

Nikayla in a mask

a bag of oxygen
over her face
features hidden
by enriched air.

Every time the body
forgets to breathe
this embarrassment

not wanting to show
her face.

iii

Randy won't hold the baby now
because once near the warmth
of his body she almost died.

No one touches her
except Janice and the nurse.

And we wait
in the corridor every evening
the hospital air cool and
dry as the exact
relation of our bodies
to our lives.

iv

To breathe
the bed throbs under her.

To breathe
you cover her face with oxygen.

To breathe
the chemicals are needled into her skin.

To breathe
(and this on the hospital's instructions)
you tickle her feet.

To breathe

you hold your breath.

v

You can hardly see her
dwarfed by the contrivances
cords, tubes, air
she pulls to herself
in red hands

and the white-smocked people
coming and going and waiting
for the signal her wired body
sends as it dies

and her body sends it.

A nurse walking over to her
to shake the air back into her.

Sue Gauthier, it says
on the nurse's pin
and I see her nipples
brown and perfect
through the light summer uniform.

vi

And a picture of Niki
on the couch
with the other kids.

Janice took the picture
one evening when Randy
was out doing some plumbing
for the neighbours.

The kids are watching tv
their faces full
of an ignorance
of pain.

To be read to Randy and Janice on Ben's birthday

The plaster deer
on the front lawn
curl up under snow.
The paint is already
chipping.

At the window
that overlooks the lawn
she reaches up to draw
the curtains.

The dream in her belly
kicks in its fluid.
The deer that vanish
under snow contain
their own walking away.

For Seven Years

The cells split and die. Our bodies
you said, remake us every seven years.
A rose is a rose.
              We never examine
our time together. We sit in the living
room with the tv on, gone to fat and stretchmarks.
Our flesh, when it regenerates, regenerates
familiar pains.
              We hang the calendar
on the wall and fill it with birthdays
anniversaries, meeting dates.
Reschedule our lives.
                 I watch you
on the couch and know there are changes
coded in your body. The hands that touch me
repeat themselves endlessly.
I want to tell you I love you I love you
the calendar is full of indifference
and glossy pictures of flowers
again.

Homecoming '79

All the people who come home are old.
In the afternoon the old men sat
in the shade beside the legion,
watched for out-of-province plates,
while the ladies served coffee and date squares
at the community hall. The old-timers
played ball and won.
All day we shake the hands of people
who knew us when we were that high;
they come home to reclaim us.
We smile and don't remember.

At night, in the weird shadows
from three bulbs strung across the ceiling
of the tent they're using for a bar
we watch the people press in
watch for a face lit by heat or
beer or ghosts, some
grin to recognize.
But there are none, except Jack
who ran a truck from Ryley to the city.
I moved these people he says
Edmonton, Medicine Hat, Flatbush . . . away.
As soon as one left they all wanted to go.
Now they're here and some of them never
did pay me. I always thought
I'd buy another truck and move
some of them home.
His hands hold on to the back of a chair
like a steering wheel and in the vague
familiarity of generations, faces our
grandparents knew, here now for the dead
myths of a small town, the conversation
hammers like an engine in the hall.

Every Year

In the slough by the trailer court
chorus frogs fit the air
into their throats and blackbirds
bloom yellow-headed, redwinged, from the
cattails. Behind us mosquitos.
Ahead of us the Army Road.
This is the third year in a row:
the long slow ride out to the meadows
east of Beaverhill Lake to see
if there are still crocuses
to watch the cranes and pelicans
to lie among the coarse grass
as the evening comes in slow
as driftwood and not to notice
any of it.

Monty Reid has lived in both Saskatchewan and Alberta, presently making his home in Camrose, Alberta. His poetry has appeared in a variety of literary publications across Canada. Previous books of Reid's poems include *Fridays* (Sidereal Press) and *Karst Means Stone* (Ne-West Press).

THISTLEDOWN BOOKS

WIND SONGS by Glen Sorestad
DARK HONEY by Ronald Marken
INSIDE IS THE SKY by Lorna Uher
OCTOMI by Andrew Suknaski
SUMMER'S BRIGHT BLOOD by William Latta
PRAIRIE PUB POEMS by Glen Sorestad
PORTRAITS by Lala Koehn
HAIL STORM by Peter Christensen
BETWEEN THE LINES by Stephen Scriver
GATHERING FIRE by Helen Hawley
TOWARDS A NEW COMPASS by Lorne Daniel
NOW IS A FAR COUNTRY by John V. Hicks
OLD WIVES LAKE by J. D. Fry
THE CURRIED CHICKEN APOCALYPSE by Michael Cullen
ANCESTRAL DANCES by Glen Sorestad
EAST OF MYLOONA by Andrew Suknaski
BLUE SUNRISE by Bert Almon
THE MUSHROOM JAR by Nancy Senior
WINTER YOUR SLEEP by John V. Hicks
DIRT HILLS MIRAGE by Barbara Sapergia
LAND OF THE PEACE by Leona Gom
RIG TALK by Peter Christensen
DISTURBANCES by Greg Simison
THE BOOK OF THIRTEEN by Gertrude Story
THE LIFE OF RYLEY by Monty Reid

Date Due